Evaluation of Achievement

Douglas A. Pidgeon

Citation Press, New York 1972

ISBN 590-09527-7
Library of Congress Catalog Card number 74-168888

This book is published simultaneously in Great
Britain, Canada and other countries of the British
Commonwealth by Macmillan Education Ltd and
in the United States by Citation Press, Library
and Trade Division Scholastic Magazines, Inc.

Designer Richard Hollis

Printed in the U.S.A.

Preface

The purpose of the Anglo-American Primary Education Project is to provide descriptions of the way that British primary schools work. They are published in this series of booklets under the general title of *Informal Schools in Britain Today* and they have been written for American and British educators and teachers-in-training as well as for the general public.

The authors are either practitioners or expert observers of British primary education and, in most cases, they document the work of the schools through detailed case examples; where it is relevant, implications are stated and conclusions drawn. It is not the intention to provide theoretical discussions or prescriptive manuals to informal education, but rather to present accounts from which deductions and generalizations can be made. In so doing, these booklets draw on the experience of that large minority of primary schools that have adopted informal methods.

It is hoped that the booklets will help educators who are looking for examples to substantiate change in particular schools and also those who are concerned, as teachers, educators or administrators, with the wider implications of the education of young children. For students who plan to become teachers these accounts of what happens in the classrooms of British primary schools provide ample material for discussion as well as helpful insights into the practice of teaching.

The series has been prepared under the aegis of the Schools Council in England with the support of the Ford Foundation in the United States. Planning was assisted by a small Anglo-American advisory group whose members are listed on page 6. The views expressed are however personal to each author.

British Directorate

Geoffrey Cockerill, Project Chairman/Joint Secretary, Schools Council for Curriculum and Examinations, London.

John Blackie/Formerly Chief Inspector, Primary Education, Department of Education and Science, London.

Molly Brearley/Formerly Principal, Froebel Institute College of Education, London.

Maurice Kogan, Project Co-ordinator/Professor of Government and Social Administration, School of Social Sciences, Brunel University, Uxbridge, Middlesex.

American Participants

J. Myron Atkin/Dean, School of Education, University of Illinois, Urbana, Illinois.

Ann Cook/Co-director, Community Resources Institute, 270 W. 96th Street, New York.

Joseph Featherstone/Writer; Lecturer, John Fitzgerald Kennedy School of Government, Institute of Politics, Harvard University, Cambridge, Massachusetts.

Professor David Hawkins/Director, Mountain View Center for Environmental Education, University of Colorado, Boulder, Colorado.

Herb Mack/Co-director, Community Resources Institute, 270 W. 96th Street, New York.

Marjorie Martus/Program Officer, The Ford Foundation, New York, N.Y.

Casey Murrow/Teacher, Wilmington Elementary School, Wilmington, Vermont.

Liza Murrow/Antioch-Putney Graduate School of Education, Putney, Vermont.

Mary Lela Sherburne/Director, Pilot Communities Project, Education Development Center, Newton, Mass.

Contents

The Author

Douglas A. Pidgeon was born in 1919. He gained a B Sc in psychology, at the University of London, in 1949. He taught in special schools for handicapped children before joining, in 1950, the staff of the National Foundation for Educational Research in England and Wales and became head of the Foundation's Test Services in 1954. He was Visiting Lecturer, Teachers College, Columbia University, 1962–3. In 1963, he was appointed deputy director of the NFER. He is a Fellow of the British Psychological Society, a member of the American Educational Research Association, and a Ph D, University of Stockholm, Sweden, 1970. He has published many articles on measurement and evaluation and is the co-author of several books on these and other related subjects.

Introduction

The considerable changes that have taken place in British primary education in the past hundred years or so offer complete verification, if such be needed, of the maxim that schools, and the education system to which they belong, reflect the views of the society which produced them.[1] Conceived in a society in which elementary education was regarded almost as a charity for the children of the poor, the Elementary Education Act of 1870, for example, laid particular stress on the curriculum to be taught and the standards to be exacted. The narrowness of the curriculum, which was confined to reading, writing and arithmetic, reflected precisely the intention of elementary education as it was then understood, and the maintenance of standards was considered essential to justify the expenditure of public money.

The meaning of elementary education had already changed before the end of the nineteenth century, partly as a result of the introduction of compulsory schooling and also because of the very effectiveness of the elementary school and the fact that many poor but clever children could outstrip the standards laid down. A large social and educational gulf existed, however, between the elementary and the secondary sectors of the system, even into the twentieth century. Later there was a similar division at the secondary level, and some would argue that this is still with us despite the introduction of comprehensive schools (Eaglesham, 1967).[2] At the primary level, however, education has been comprehensive, in most senses of the term, for very many years, and this has influenced to a considerable degree many of the changes which have taken place.

[1] See, in this series, AN INTRODUCTION by Joseph Featherstone

[2] As there are a large number of bibliographical references in this booklet, they have not, as in other booklets in this series, been given in footnotes. They will be found in the Bibliography (pages 40–2)

The early changes were almost entirely concerned with the content of the curriculum—first with a broadening from the restrictions of the three Rs, and then, as a unified State system of elementary education developed in the latter part of the nineteenth century, with a sounder preparation for what was to become secondary education for all. But the stress remained largely on the curriculum content, and the process of education was still regarded by many as one solely of instruction, in which the teacher imparted knowledge to the pupils he had to teach. What had to be conveyed was, more or less, agreed upon, and pupils fitted into the requirements of the school as best they could.

Under such a system as this, evaluation was relatively straightforward. Provided agreement could be reached on what pupils at any particular age-level were expected to know, the task of ascertaining how many in fact reached it did not present any special difficulty. Not that deliberate evaluation was in fact undertaken, except perhaps during the famous 'payment by results' era.[1] We now look back with undisguised disapproval on this period in British education, yet, if it is regarded within the social context of the time, it will be seen as an exercise in evaluation on a national scale that has hardly been equalled even into modern times.

The aims of elementary education in the middle of the nineteenth century were clearly understood —that children should learn to read, write and do arithmetic. Moreover, with its Revised Code of 1862, the Education Department specified the precise standards to be reached after each year of schooling. A child completing his first year in Standard 1, for example, should be able to read 'a short paragraph from a book used in the school not confined to words of one syllable', to 'copy in manuscript character a line of print and write from dictation a few common words' and, in arithmetic to be able to carry out 'simple addition and subtraction of numbers of not more than four figures and the multiplication table of 6 times 12'.

[1] From 1863 to 1898, part of a teacher's salary was dependent on the success of children in his class, in an annual examination conducted by Her Majesty's Inspectors of schools. (See, in this series, THE GOVERNMENT OF EDUCATION by Maurice Kogan)

8

The Education Department of the time wanted some clear evidence that these aims and objectives were being achieved in order to be able to justify the expenditure of public money on State education. The Newcastle Commission Report of 1861 described how this could be done by instituting 'a searching examination by competent authority of every child in every school to which grants are paid'. The actual assessment was carried out by Her Majesty's Inspectors, who conscientiously attempted to apply the same standard from school to school.

After the ending of 'payment by results' in 1898, there was no further formal attempt at systematic evaluation. With our present-day sophistication in evaluation techniques we may condemn the narrowness of the aims of education as then set out, and criticize the subjectivity of the methods used to evaluate them, but we should at least applaud the correctness of the procedure followed—first, considering the aims of education, and second, proceeding to evaluate the achievement of those aims.

The ending of the 'payment by results' era heralded further changes. Teachers were no longer bound to a specified curriculum but were given greater freedom not only to define their own syllabuses but also to vary teaching methods. Initially the stress was still on the syllabus, or on the methods and materials to be used in teaching it, but in the years leading up to the 1944 Education Act, other influences were at work which brought about a change in emphasis from concern with the subject matter and its teaching to concern about the child as a learner. The educational process was regarded less as one in which the teacher imparted knowledge and more as one in which the individual child learned at his own pace and in his own way. The 1944 Act built this change into the statutes by omitting any reference to what kind of instruction a child was to receive and merely stating that he was to be educated according to his age, ability and aptitude. It might be noted, at this point, that this change was bound to have considerable repercussions on any process of evaluation. No longer would it be possible to state, even in imprecise terms, what the State required from the education system for which it was paying. Children, it was now recognized, varied enormously in their abilities and aptitudes—and, it might be added, in their interests and aspirations as well—and from now on it was not going to be easy to define in simple terms what it was they were all expected to learn at any given age.

Evaluation, of course, did not stop completely in 1898. HM Inspectors were no longer required to act as examiners, but they continued for many years to be influential in the maintenance of standards. However as the autonomy of schools in matters concerning the curriculum increased and standardized tests became available to primary school teachers, even this function lessened and HMIs began to play a more dominant role in the introduction of innovation and change itself.

An historical summary, in this context, is necessarily brief. It is not the purpose of this booklet either to list the changes that have taken or are taking place within the British primary school, or to describe in any detail the factors which were instrumental in bringing them about; rather the concern is with the question of what effect they are having. Nevertheless, it is relevant to note that the changes which have occurred have been largely the result of changes in the attitudes of teachers, induced in part, perhaps, by the more liberal attitudes to education which prevailed in the early part of the twentieth century. That such changes have occurred in British primary schools is undoubtedly due to the greater freedom which they enjoy compared with schools in most other countries. The freedom is not complete, however, and external examinations have always exercised strong controlling pressures, except in the infant schools, and this is perhaps the reason why innovation and experimentation started in these schools.[1]

The infant school demonstrated what was possible, and if the spread of ideas upwards into the junior school was slow, this can be attributed both to the commendable conservatism of teachers, who rightly resist a change from well-known and well-tried methods to those unfamiliar and untried, and to the restricting influence of the eleven-plus examination. With the coming of comprehensive education at the secondary level, and with it, in many areas, the disappearance of the need for selection, the pace of change at the junior level is undoubtedly accelerating.

Any attempt that might be made to evaluate the British primary school is necessarily complicated by the fact that teacher attitudes and expectations have an important part to play in determining pupil achievement. (Evidence of this is documented in the Appendix to this booklet.) Labels are readily attached to the many innovations and new techniques which are becoming increasingly popular in schools—vertical or family grouping,[2] team-teaching, programmed instruction, teaching machines, etc—but these in themselves are, or should be, only symptomatic of more important changes of attitude in the teachers using them. Quite often attempts to evaluate them are made as though innovations themselves are the sole instruments of change. Many such innovations are, however, merely introduced as adjuncts to traditional teaching methods, with no corresponding changes in the beliefs and attitudes of the teachers concerned. Evaluation studies which do not take into account the different views of teachers, or which fail to incorporate into their design differences in teacher behaviour stemming from differently held beliefs, may well fail to provide any real evidence of the effects of change. This point can be easily demonstrated with reference to the problem of 'streaming' or homogeneous ability-grouping. Countless attempts to evaluate streaming failed largely because two important factors were consistently omitted from

[1] See, in this series, FROM HOME TO SCHOOL by Alice Murton

[2] See, in this series, SPACE, TIME AND GROUPING by Richard Palmer

the studies—the attitudes and beliefs of the teachers concerned, and the classroom practices which stemmed from these (Goldberg, Passow and Justman, 1966, and Barker Lunn, 1970). Barker Lunn, in her investigation, was able to measure teachers' attitudes, in her study of such things as eleven-plus selection, bright and backward children and, of course, streaming. In addition, information was obtained on a number of teaching practices, such as the seating arrangement employed, the use of class, group or individual teaching methods, and the setting of the formal traditional, or informal, more progressive type of lesson. An analysis of the results of these measurements enabled two types of teacher to be identified—those who, in their attitudes and beliefs and classroom practices, supported streaming and those who did not. Teachers of both types were found in each kind of organization, streamed and unstreamed. Barker Lunn's results provided evidence that these basic characteristics of the teachers were more important in determining many of the schools' outcomes than was the actual method of organization.

Similarly, it is suggested that the success of the many approaches now being followed in primary schools is likely to depend far more upon the individual teachers using them than upon any organizational change in itself. Unless, therefore, relevant aspects of the teachers' philosophy and attitudes, as well as specific features of the learning situation created by the new approaches, are taken into account, evaluations will be as varied and inconsistent as were those from the early studies of streaming. Blanket comparisons of outcomes from schools using new approaches with those not so doing, will prove of very limited value.

1 Problems in Evaluation—Aims

It is clear from what has already been said that an evaluation of the British primary school cannot be easily undertaken. Yet it is only sensible that some attempt should be made to assess whether the monumental changes now taking place are really producing the results desired. If the result of the evaluation carried out by HM Inspectors in the latter half of the nineteenth century was indeed a justification of the public money spent on education, is the same likely to be true today? Even allowing for greater numbers, and for changes in the value of money, the amount spent on primary schooling in this country has increased tremendously over the past fifty years or so. Are children receiving a better education than they did fifty years ago? Or is it possible that some of the changes are the result of the passing whims and fancies of fashionable educationists and psychologists, and despite appearances basic standards are really falling? The publication of the recent series of BLACK PAPERS (Cox and Dyson, 1969, 1970) is evidence enough that these are serious and important questions which merit careful consideration, and any attempt to answer them needs to go beyond exacting a definition of what is meant by 'a better education' and by 'basic standards'.

One generally accepted pattern of development and evaluation has three stages: first, specifying the aims and objectives to be achieved; second, devising the materials, methods and approaches appropriate for their achievement; and third, evaluating the extent to which the aims have been achieved. However, in practice, such a pattern is rarely found—perhaps only in specially-designed curriculum development studies. In practice, the second stage often takes place before the first; that is, changes are made before the aims implied by them are stated. Indeed, for the evaluator looking at the modern scene, this is exactly what has happened over the last hundred years, with two added complications: first, that the changes that have taken place are directed at different sets of aims, and second, that the changes themselves, and what is implied by them, are by no means universally accepted.

Differences in aims

The first complication creates more difficulties for the evaluator, although the second is not without its problems. Changes which entail a move away from the didactic approach to one which involves children more actively in the learning process were first given official blessing in the HADOW PRIMARY SCHOOL REPORT (Board of Education Consultative Committee, 1931). As has been pointed out, the rate of change is accelerating and the publication of the Plowden Report must have done a great deal to encourage the less enthusiastic teacher to depart from the main traditional methods of teaching. Even so, it is probably still only a minority of the nation's primary schools that can truly be termed 'progressive'—in the sense that they adopted approaches that can be given labels such as 'free day', 'integrated day', 'informal school', etc. Rogers gives an estimate of about twenty-five per cent of schools in the 'progressive' category, with forty per cent 'quite traditional' and another thirty per cent or so 'in various stages of transition' (Rogers, 1970). No recent systematic survey has in fact been carried out, but contact with fairly large numbers of schools participating in research projects for the NFER[1] tends to confirm the view that the figure of twenty-five per cent ('progressive' schools) given by Rogers is probably an over-estimate. It follows that any statements made about the aims of education in the more progressive schools do not

[1]The National Foundation for Educational Research in England and Wales, is an independent research organization, financed largely by funds supplied by local education authorities, teacher organizations and the Department of Education and Science

14

necessarily apply to all primary schools.

It is, of course, no more than a statement of the obvious to assert that no evaluation is possible until precisely what it is that has to be evaluated is known. Evaluation, after all, is a procedure aimed at discovering the extent to which previously determined aims are being achieved. If aims have been clearly stated *before* the means of achieving them have been developed, the evaluator has a relatively easy task—at least he knows what he has to assess. On the other hand, if aims have not been stated at the outset, it is clear that the task of determining them has first priority. Any discussion of evaluation in the British primary school must therefore start with an examination of its aims. Before turning to this, however, there are two further points which need some clarification.

Facts and value judgements

First it is important to distinguish between facts and value judgements. Good evaluation rests much more on objectively collected facts than on subjective opinion. Yet human judgement necessarily enters into even good evaluation. At two points, at the beginning and at the end, no matter how accurately and objectively the facts have been collected, decisions need to be made. The decision made at the beginning of the evaluation is perhaps the more difficult, since it involves the choice of what aims are to be assessed and what priorities are to be adopted. Evaluation, of course, must be concerned with all possible aims. It is as important to know what is not being achieved as to know what is. But a person who wishes to know whether the primary schools of today are 'better' than those of fifty years ago, must be prepared to specify exactly in terms of which, of all possible aims, he is expecting it to be 'better'. And he must justify the decision he makes. Anyone, for example, who argues that it is more important for nine-year-olds to know their multiplication tables than to have inquiring mathematical minds, or to write neatly and spell accurately than to express themselves imaginatively, must be prepared to back his judgements.

The value of judgement at the end of an evaluation is not unconnected with that at the beginning. It involves judging how much is good enough. If sixty per cent of children achieve a stated objective, can the schools concerned be said to be successful? If comparisons with previous years are available—percentages achieving a known score on a particular test of reading for example—there is little problem. However if the aim to be evaluated is one concerning, say, the development of certain attitudes in society, and appropriate measures are produced and used, then a judgement must inevitably be involved, in deciding the 'pass mark', and deciding what percentage of positive attitudes will be regarded as acceptable.

In Britain, the aims of education are, in the last resort, determined by the general public, whose elected representatives enact legislation to govern the educational process.[1] This legislation, and the associated documents, lay down the broad lines of policy that are to be followed. But the language used in the legislation is necessarily rather vague and general, and, while the associated documents are somewhat more specific, a large area of important detail remains subject to local option, whether exercised again by the general public in their capacity as local government electors or by those charged with the duty of actually organizing and running the schools. Thus, to say, as does the 1944 Education Act, that children are to be educated in accordance with their age, ability and aptitude, and in accordance with the wishes of their parents, is a declaration of principle that requires much interpretation to reduce to practice. For example, it could imply that all children are to have an equal share of the available resources. Or that the parable of the sower is to be followed, and that those who profit most from the early stages should receive a larger share later on. Or again, it could imply the opposite, or compensatory principle.

[1] See, in this series, THE GOVERNMENT OF EDUCATION by Maurice Kogan

Objectives of primary education

There is no doubt that the problems of evaluating the British primary school would be very much simpler if there were universal agreement on the aims and objectives of primary education. But, as has already been stated, schools inevitably reflect the views of the society in which they exist, and at this moment in time, society itself is in a state of flux, and hence widely disparate views are held on what kind of structure society itself should have. Since the overriding purpose of any education system must be to prepare children for the society in which as adults they will take their place, it would appear to follow that there must exist a variety of aims and objectives in the schools. It might be argued, for example, that an education aimed to fit a child of low ability and social status into his allotted place in a hierarchical society would necessarily be quite different from one which aimed to equip him to live in a fully egalitarian society. In the former it might be appropriate for him to be instructed in a homogeneous ability-group whereas in the latter it would not. The aims of education, therefore, are necessarily spread over a comparatively wide front and it would be difficult to reach agreement on what they should be, except in the broadest terms. From the point of view of evaluation, such an exercise would, in any case, be valueless. It is only possible to ascertain whether or not something is being achieved, if that something can be stated in clear unequivocal operational terms.

A detailed list of all possible objectives of primary education does not, of course, exist, although such a list would be necessary if any attempt to carry out a total evaluation of primary education were contemplated. It would also be necessary to know what priorities should be attached to the objectives. Is it more important, for example, that children should know how to calculate the area of a room than that they should develop an attitude of acceptance and tolerance of minority groups? Or should these objectives be given equal weight? Not even a partial evaluation can be carried out without

17

this kind of information. It might, for example, be agreed that a specific type of programme (such as guided discovery learning) being followed in a number of schools is aiming to achieve a specified set of objectives (including, for example, the ability to solve unseen problems in mathematics). It would be a reasonably straightforward task to ascertain the extent to which the stated objectives were being achieved. But such an evaluation would have limitations. It would also be important to know whether other objectives (such as, for example, knowledge of the multiplication tables) which had not been specified by this particular programme, but which nevertheless were regarded by some people as important, were also being achieved. The problem, of course, is who is to specify the 'other' objectives and decide what they should be. Value judgements enter here, and different people have different values.

Changes in values Values also change over time. For example, over the past ten years or so, there has been an increase in the proportion of teachers who believe that children are more likely to write well in the long run if they are at first encouraged to write freely about topics on which they have something spontaneous to say than if they are checked by being called on to correct mistakes. This is on the principle that 'those who are afraid to make mistakes will make little'. However this may be, it is plain that free writers will be very apt to make mistakes in the early stages, and may therefore do rather badly on an old-fashioned test that counts their vices and not their virtues. This is analogous to the difficulty of assessing changes in the cost of living. Some of the cost of living today is in respect of goods and services that did not exist in past times. In the same way, changes in the content of the curriculum make direct comparison with past times over a wide area relatively difficult if not impossible.

2 Problems in Evaluation—Methods

A number of the problems and difficulties associated with any evaluation have been mentioned here, not just to expose the difficulty of the task but in order to indicate the limitations which must be held in mind when the results of evaluations are being interpreted. In practice, evidence of the efficiency of the British primary school can come either from a specific investigation undertaken with evaluation in mind, or from the results of researches and surveys initiated for other purposes. Obviously the former is likely to produce more results of direct value than the latter, but unfortunately, from an examination of published and on-going studies, it is clear that no comprehensive evaluation either has been or is being carried out. Many of the more material aspects of change have been selected for study, such as teaching machines, family grouping, programmed instruction and team teaching. The NFER's list of current researches (NFER, 1970) shows forty such studies in progress at the moment, but in none of these, it would seem, is any systematic attempt being made to measure and control such important aspects as teacher attitudes. Studies of this kind aim more to evaluate the effectiveness of the instruments of change than what is implied by the change itself.

Specific evaluation

With all the extensive changes now taking place, it is clear that only an evaluation specifically designed to discover the extent to which a variety of objectives is being met is likely to produce the kind of evidence that will satisfy protagonists and antagonists alike. Such a study would have to be carried out on a carefully selected sample of schools which represented the best and the worst of both the traditional and the newer informal approaches to teaching and learning. The aims and objectives of the sample schools should cover not only those aspects of education which are given more emphasis with the informal approach, but also those which the critics of change hold in high esteem. Furthermore, the evaluation should concern itself not only with assessing this wide variety of output but should also include suitable measures of input and process variables. The backgrounds and abilities which the children bring with them when they come to school are clearly important as are the attitudes and beliefs of the teachers concerned.

Until a specially designed study is carried out, evidence relating to the effectiveness of any changed approach in the primary school must be sought from other sources. Such a procedure is obviously far from ideal and the danger must always exist that invalid conclusions will be drawn. Care must therefore be exercised in interpreting data obtained from other than a comprehensive evaluation study, and their limitations kept well in mind.

Surveys of attainment   One source of evidence on which comparisons of primary schools following different approaches might be made is the periodic survey of attainment. One recommendation of the Plowden Report was, indeed, that recurring surveys should be carried out (paragraph 554), and, on the basic subject of reading evidence is indeed available from surveys carried out since 1948. Before setting out the available evidence, however, it is necessary to stress the major limitation of such survey data—namely that they are assessing only the outcomes of cognitive learning and, however much these may be regarded as important, especially in such a basic subject as reading, nevertheless, as has been stressed, the affective side of learning must not be totally ignored.

The direct comprehension of reading is a relatively
straightforward matter, and a large measure of
agreement can be reached on its measurement—a
fact which is fortunate in view of its importance.
The evidence from the periodic surveys carried out
by the Department of Education and Science between 1948 and 1964 have been fully reported (DES,
1966). For children in primary schools the following
table gives the results succinctly:

Table 1

Percentile scores for pupils aged eleven

Rank %	1948	1952	1956	1964
90	18.4	19.5	21.1	22.8
80	15.9	16.8	18.8	20.5
70	14.2	15.1	16.7	18.4
60	12.7	13.6	14.7	16.4
50	11.3	12.2	13.0	14.7
40	9.8	10.7	11.3	13.0
30	8.1	9.0	9.6	11.3
20	6.6	7.2	7.9	9.4
10	3.9	4.9	5.6	7.5
Mean Score	11.6	12.4	13.3	15.0

The average gain in score over the sixteen years
is shown in the lowest row of Table 1 as 3.4 points. It
is apparent from the body of the table that over
most of the range a point of score is equivalent to
about six percentile ranks. Consequently the gain
of 3.4 points is equivalent to about 20 percentile
ranks. For example, a score of 11.3 represented the
fiftieth rank in 1948, but only the thirtieth rank in
1964. Another way of representing the gain is to
note that, for pupils aged eleven, a point of score is
equivalent to five months of reading age, so that
the gain of 3.4 is equivalent to an improvement

of about seventeen months of reading age.

The strength of the progress illustrated by the table above can be considered under two heads. These are the accuracy of the sampling and the appropriateness of the test. The questions are practically independent. The accuracy of the sampling would need to be demonstrated whatever the test, and the appropriateness of the test would need to be considered whatever the accuracy of the sampling—and, indeed, even if every child in the whole country had been tested.

The essence of fairness in sampling is to make the draw by giving each member of the target population a specifiable chance of appearing in the sample. The chances need not be equal, but if they are unequal, differential weighting is needed in compensation. Provided that the draw is made in this way, the accuracy or representativeness of the sample can be assessed from the internal evidence that it contains. This can be done by working out the standard error of any estimate needed from the sample. The table below gives the standard errors for the mean scores in the various surveys.

Table 2

Mean Scores—Pupils aged eleven

1948	1952	1956	1964
11.59 (0.59)	12.42 (0.30)	13.30 (0.32)	15.00 (0.21)

The 1948 sample was treated as if it were a probability sample, although it was in fact a judgement sample. The reason for its large standard error is that it was a three-stage sample, with only a small number (four) of local education authorities. The 1952 sample was based on fifteen local authorities, and the 1956 sample on twenty-three. The sample of 1964 was a two-stage sample, with schools drawn directly from the whole country. The figures in Table 2 demonstrate that, with a careful sampling design, reliable estimates of national averages for an age group can be obtained from samples containing only one pupil in four hundred.

The general nature of the reading test (known as the Watts-Vernon) used in all the surveys is that it consists of thirty-five questions, increasing rapidly in difficulty. For each question, the pupil has to select the right answer from five given words. The early questions are so simple that almost any pupil can answer them if they are put to him orally, so that, if a pupil fails to answer them, it is reasonable to think that this is because he cannot read them. On the other hand, a pupil may have mastered the mechanics of reading, and still be quite unable to obtain a high score because he lacks the vocabulary, general knowledge and understanding needed to grasp the meaning and give the answer when he is confronted by the later questions. At one end, the test answers the questions 'Can he read at all?', and, at the other end, the question 'Can he read to some purpose, like an educated man?'

If this test were to be used as the sole measure of the ability of a particular child, it could very properly be objected that, whatever factors guided the choice of question, in the last resort one question must be given preference in selection over another, and that this will make for a random distribution of good and bad fortune among the children who subsequently take the test. But it is the essence of randomness that it tends to cancel out over large numbers, and the object of the surveys is not to make judgements about individuals, but to assess the progress of populations, by means of samples large enough for the good and bad luck to cancel out. Even where the distribution of good and bad fortune is not random, the effects are eliminated provided the proportions remain the same. This is strikingly illustrated by the constancy of the bias of the test in favour of boys, which has been very steady, at about one point, from the beginning. Analysis has shown that the bias lies almost entirely in nine of the questions, with one of them accounting for more than a fifth of the total. This is a case where the distribution of luck implied by the choice of question is known not to be random, but to favour one sex. But because the favour is constant it does not invalidate the comparison of one year with another.

These arguments go some way to suggest that different methods of assessing average progress will lead to much the same conclusions over a moderate period of time. The arguments in favour of the test used in these surveys are: first, that it implies a definition of reading ability that is in accordance with common sense, and, secondly, that it takes no more than ten minutes of the pupil's time. A strong argument against its continual use, however, is that evidence of consistency over sixteen years does not imply consistency over a longer period. The vocabulary and ideas that make up the questions in the test must inevitably, with time, become outdated, and hence the decline of a point or two in average score may not necessarily mean a lowering of average reading standards, but merely that for many children the difficulty of some of the questions has changed.

Over the period covered by the results shown above, the rise in average score has in fact, been remarkably consistent. The gain is 3.4 points over the sixteen years, and it is made up of 0.8 and 0.9 for the first two periods of four years, together with 1.7 for the final period of eight years. Despite this, however, for a repeat of the survey carried out by the National Foundation for Educational Research in 1970, the question of the suitability of the test was considered at some length. On two counts it was decided that, although the Watts-Vernon test would be used to enable comparisons to be made with previous results, a second test would also be given to a similarly constituted probability sample This decision was taken because, despite precautions, the Watts-Vernon test was beginning to get known in the schools—a factor which would tend to raise the scores—and because a number of the brighter children (particularly at the age of fifteen, where the test was also used) were getting maximum scores, implying that with more difficult items they might have done better—a factor which would tend to depress the scores. How much these two factors were operating was unknown—hence the decision to change the test. It was also recognized that, despite the worthy service it had given, the test was becoming somewhat outdated.

The evidence given here, from the surveys, is certainly encouraging. Two points must, however, be considered. In the first place, they only start in 1948, and a comment frequently made is that the post-war recovery may only have regained what was in fact lost under the very trying circumstances in which schools had to operate during the war. In the second place, the surveys have not covered the last half-dozen years, during which time the changes in primary schools have increased significantly.

The difficulty about taking comparisons back to an earlier period is that before 1952 there were no properly constructed national samples in this or any other country. Burt, it is true, has published evidence (Burt, 1969) derived from small judgement samples of ten schools in inner London, as follows:

Table 3
Mean Scores—Inner London Sample (Burt)

Date	Reading Comp.	Reading Accuracy	Spelling	Mechanical Arithmetic	Problem Arithmetic	Mean
1914	100.0	100.0	100.0	100.0	100.0	100.0
1917	96.4	94.0	92.1	88.3	91.3	92.4
1920	99.9	98.6	97.3	96.9	98.7	98.3
1930	95.1	99.3	97.3	100.0	93.5	99.0
1945	93.3	93.3	87.1	85.9	92.0	90.3
1955	97.8	93.8	91.3	88.6	94.3	93.2
1965	99.3	95.4	92.0	92.5	96.3	95.1

The first column shows a substantial gain in reading comprehension from 1945 to 1965 although when allowance is made for the scales of the two tests used, this gain is only two thirds of the gain shown by the national samples from 1948 to 1964. This is in line with the findings of the survey of reading comprehension carried out in the Inner London Education Authority (ILEA, 1969), which gives 94 as the mean score for eight-year-olds on a test recently standardized nationally to a mean of 100 and a standard deviation of 15. Inner London suffered heavily from bombing, and now contains a very large proportion of recent immigrants whose command of English is generally rather poor, so that on both counts it seems likely that substantial adjustments would be needed to make the inner London figures representative of the country as a whole. In other words, although Burt's inner London chain shows 1965 at the same level, for reading comprehension, as 1914, it may well be that, over the country as a whole, there has been a net gain of half a dozen points or more.

On the other hand, it seems quite likely that the relativities between the different tests shown in the lowest row of Table 3, or something like them, would hold for the country as a whole, because of changes of stress in the curriculum. No one doubts the importance of reading comprehension but spelling and mechanical arithmetic are less highly valued in the majority of schools today than they were in 1914. There is argument about whether this is a good thing, but not about whether it is a fact. Consequently it is to be expected that, in comparison with 1914, relatively low scores would be obtained in these tests, more particularly since their form has not been changed during the half century that has elapsed. The question here is rather analogous to that involved in the cost of living index. Not only do the prices of goods and services change with time. The quantities, and the kinds of goods and services that enter into the cost of living also change. If spelling and mechanical arithmetic have advanced less in the whole country since 1914, this fact need not be regretted if it is outweighed by advances in other directions.

The fact that the national reading surveys do not go beyond 1964 will, of course, be rectified when the NFER 1970 survey results are published. It is not possible to predict what this will reveal. Apart from the factors already mentioned concerning the suitability of the Watts-Vernon test, other changes have taken place which could exert an influence on the mean reading score obtained. A considerable number of infant and junior schools have taken to the use of the initial teaching alphabet as a medium through which beginners learn to read, and this may well have influenced the reading performances of many of the eleven-year-olds tested in 1970. Also, during the 1960s, many primary schools received an influx of immigrant children whose knowledge of English was either non-existent or extremely limited, and this, too, must inevitably have affected the national average. Additional information on the medium of instruction (initial teaching alphabet or traditional orthography) employed, and the native language and period of residence in England, has been obtained for most children in the NFER survey, and this may help to demonstrate the possible influence of these factors. Unfortunately, no measures were obtained of the other changes with which this booklet is largely concerned, such as the attitudes and approaches of the teachers involved. Hence it will not be possible to derive estimates of the possible influence which such factors might exert. A continued rise in national standards into 1970 can therefore be viewed with some satisfaction, whereas a halt in the rise, or even a slight decline, cannot be interpreted as being necessarily due to the development of the informal school.

Surveys in other subjects If there are problems in utilizing the evidence from national reading surveys for the specific purpose of comparing formally and informally structured primary schools, there can be no doubt about their usefulness for checking trends in over-all standards. The possibility that similar surveys could be carried out in other subjects—especially mathematics—must be given careful consideration. As was illustrated by the data provided by Burt, however, mathematics, in particular, presents a much more difficult problem. Changes are taking place not only in the attitude to its learning but also in the very structure of the subject itself, and wide variations in how it is being taught exist in different primary schools. If the instructional objectives of learning to read are fairly straightforward, the same cannot be said for mathematics, and it is no easy matter to devise a simple test that can be used to carry out a survey similar to that in reading. For example, the school which emphasizes the ability to calculate and solve simple problems might do badly on a test which demanded a conceptual understanding of the basic arithmetical processes and some insight into the mathematical structure of the everyday world. In the same way, a school which stresses these latter aspects, taking the view, perhaps, that machines can now take the drudgery out of calculation, and that a foundation of this kind is a better preparation for a deeper study of mathematics at the secondary school level, might do badly on a routine test of 'mechanical' and 'problem' arithmetic.

Quite clearly, the range of objectives covering mathematics learning at the end of the primary school today is so wide that it would be impossible to ask any individual pupil to take a test which aimed to measure them all. Fortunately, this is not necessary. Just as pupils can be sampled for a survey, so can items be sampled for any single test. If a pool or bank of items is prepared, covering, as adequately as possible, the totality of objectives taught in all schools, then the bank can be exhaustively sampled to produce a number of different tests of suitable length which can be given to random samples of pupils. Any one pupil would take only one test, but, provided an adequate sampling design were adopted, the results could be aggregated to determine an average score over all items. Such a procedure would necessarily entail some pupils being asked to complete a few items measuring aspects of the subject they had not been taught, but, equally, other pupils would be more lucky. Over all pupils and items, injustices would cancel out. A scheme employing principles of this kind is used in the American National Assessment of Educational Progress (Finley and Berdie, 1970) and, in Britain, details for developing a suitable bank of items, and for carrying out a nationwide survey along the lines suggested here, have been prepared and the scheme is likely to be put into operation within the next year or two.

National sample surveys of this kind can theoretically be extended to other areas of the curriculum, including the non-cognitive. The greatest practical difficulty is not the construction of an appropriate series of tests, although not all the problems of measurement are by any means solved, but obtaining agreement on the specification of the total range of objectives to be covered. Human judgement is involved here; what is not included will clearly not contribute to the evaluation, but the very exclusion of some aspects of the curriculum—such as some of the attitudinal components of school learning—involves a declaration about values on which perhaps, at this moment in time, society may not be able to reach agreement. And the dangers of restricting the areas covered by any national survey are no less than those of including too much.

Assessing the primary schools   Evaluative evidence, from national surveys, of the success or otherwise of the changes that are taking place in the British primary school is, at this point in time, extremely limited. The results of the reading surveys would give no ground for pessimism, however, even if they do not supply wholehearted support for the reformers. Is there any other source

of evidence which could be explored? How do th
standards achieved in England, for example, com
pare with those in other countries? Internationa
comparisons are not readily made and most of th
little evidence that has been published has been con
fined to the secondary school level. The surve
currently being undertaken by the Internationa
Association for the Evaluation of Educationa
Achievement (IEA) has included the testing in bot:
science and reading comprehension of ten- t.
eleven-year-old pupils. The results, which are du
to be published in 1972, should enable the perfor
mances, in these subject areas, of primary schoc
pupils in England to be compared with those c
their contemporaries in about a score of othe
countries around the world.

The first IEA survey was concerned wit
mathematics and here, as far as boys and girls i:
the thirteen-year-old age division were concerned
England occupied a middle place in a compac
group comprising the Netherlands, Australia
Germany, Scotland and France; well below Japar
Israel, and Belgium, but equally well above th
United States, Sweden, and Finland (Husen, 1967)
There are many factors which have to be con
sidered in interpreting evidence of this kind
including an appreciation of the differences in th
structure of the education systems concerned, bu
it would appear that, at least in mathematics, th
performance of secondary school pupils in Englan
did not compare too unfavourably with that i
other countries. This fact, coupled with the grea
increase in numbers of pupils taking public exam
inations in English secondary schools, woul
suggest a reasonable efficiency of the primar
schools, if it could be demonstrated that success a
the secondary level is, to a large extent, dependen
upon what happens in the earlier years.

In fact, in the past decade or so, an increasing
amount of evidence which supports this common
sense view has been forthcoming (eg, Bloom, 1964
Coleman *et al*, 1966). In particular the follow-up o

the primary school pupils involved in the Plowden survey (Peaker, 1967) provides clear evidence of the importance of the early years. The main finding of this study (Peaker, 1971) was that, on the average, for the four secondary-school age and sex groups concerned, data, collected in 1964, on variables concerned with the home background and the primary schools, accounted for sixty-six per cent of the variation in school performance, and data on other secondary school variables, collected in 1968, could add only seven per cent to this. Such evidence suggests that the prospect of countering the effects of an unfavourable home background is brighter in early childhood than later on; it emphasizes the importance of the primary years and provides a strong argument in favour of nursery schooling.

Direct evidence of the efficiency of the new British primary school, compared with the more traditional approach to primary education, is certainly in short supply, and the need for carefully planned and executed studies is clear enough. Until a more precise evaluation has taken place, however, it will be necessary to rely upon the more indirect kind of evidence presented here. In the long run, as has been pointed out, the beliefs and attitudes of teachers will predominate, and teachers who change to a new approach as an act of faith, because they believe it is right, will make it succeed. The real danger, and one to be guarded against, is that some teachers will make material changes in order to be fashionable, and will have little appreciation or understanding of the deeper issues involved.

Appendix

The importance of teachers' attitudes

Evidence from recent research has lent support t the view that just as, in the home environment, th attitudes of parents play a more important par than the material circumstances (Wiseman, 1964 Peaker, 1967), so too, within the school, the par played by the attitudes of teachers—and the class room practices they adopt as a result of thos attitudes—may prove to be far more importan than the more material factors such as school build ings, size of class, apparatus provided, or tech niques employed.

One area where the importance of teache attitudes may be seen is that of sex differences i the teaching of mathematics. The societal view held in many countries, that mathematics is strict ly a subject for boys, and that they are inherentl more capable than girls at achieving success in it is undoubtedly shared by many teachers. There i evidence, however, both at the primary leve (Daniels, 1959) and secondary level (Dale, 1962) tha girls in co-educational schools achieve a greate success in the subject than they do in single-se schools. A similar finding for whole countries wa reported in the IEA study (Husen, 1967). Othe factors besides attitudes may be operating here, bu this evidence certainly suggests that when girls ar taught in an atmosphere where the traditiona female suspicion of mathematics is less noticeabl and where, perhaps, the teachers are less incline to doubt their abilities in the subject, they mak greater advances than they would otherwise have done.

A further, perhaps more direct, example of th way in which the attitudes of teachers influenc their pupils' levels of performance is provided b

Burstall. In a study concerned with the teaching of French to children of primary school age, she developed and administered a scale which measured the attitudes of teachers concerned with the teaching of French to children of low ability. It is interesting to note in passing that the teachers ranged widely in their attitudes from the twenty-five per cent who considered that 'teaching French to low-ability children was a criminal waste of time', to the twenty per cent who—possibly appreciating the fact that, in France, even the dullest child in school could learn to speak French quite fluently—believed that there was no reason why the less able children in English schools should not 'learn French as well as anyone else' (Burstall, 1968). After a period of two years, all the children concerned in the investigation were given a listening comprehension test of French, and the low-ability children (arbitrarily defined by their scoring below minus-one standard deviation on other attainment tests) were divided into categories. A high-scoring group consisted of those scoring above the mean for all children, and a low-scoring group consisted of those who scored below minus-one standard deviation. The latter were not randomly distributed throughout the experimental sample, but were found to be concentrated in a small number of schools where the teachers had expressed a negative attitude towards the teaching of French to low-ability children. In a similar manner, the high-scoring, low-ability children were found concentrated in those schools where the teachers had expressed more positive attitudes.

A further finding from this same study is also of interest. It was found that the low-ability children reached the highest level of achievement in French when they had been taught in heterogeneous groups with teachers holding favourable attitudes. The most detrimental circumstances appeared to be a combination of homogeneous ability-grouping and negative teacher attitudes. In commenting on these results, Burstall says, 'In a complex of factors determining a pupil's achievement, it must surely be recognized that the teacher's attitudes and expectations are of paramount importance. We readily accept that curriculum change cannot be effected without the wholehearted involvement of the teacher; we are perhaps less ready to recognize that changes in the curriculum, no matter how far-reaching, will have little effect on the pupil from whom the teacher expects—and obtains—a low level of achievement' (Burstall, 1970).

These research findings not only demonstrate the influence that teacher attitudes can have on pupil performance, but they also suggest ways in which this influence operates. The theory that in many, if not most, situations people tend to do what is expected of them—so much so that even a false expectation may evoke the behaviour that makes it seem true—has been termed the 'self-fulfilling prophecy' (Merton, 1957). Shaw recognizes that attitudes could be more important than material circumstances, when he makes Eliza Doolittle explain to Colonel Pickering:

You see, really and truly, apart from the things anyone can pick up (the dressing and the proper way of speaking and so on), the difference between a lady and a flower girl is not how she behaves, but how she's treated. I shall always be a flower girl to Professor Higgins because he always treats me as a flower girl, and always will; but I know I can be a lady to you because you always treat me as a lady, and always will.

How teacher expectations operate with deprived children has been described by Marburger (1963):

The teacher who expects achievement, who has hope for the educability of his pupils indeed conveys this through every nuance and subtlety of his behaviour. The teacher who conveys hopelessness for the educability of his children usually does so without ever really verbalizing such an attitude—at least not in front of his pupils.

34

Ravitz (1963) also observed the self-fulfilling prophecy operating with children in slum schools:

The children were not encouraged to learn very much; the teacher expended little energy on anything but maintaining order and bemoaning her lot; as a consequence, the children fulfilled the low expectation which in turn reinforced the original assumption to prove the teacher was right.

While the self-fulfilling prophecy can be considered a reasonable hypothesis, attempts to prove it experimentally have not met with much success. The most dramatic study purporting to demonstrate that children's performances followed the expectations of their teacher is that by Rosenthal and Jacobson (1968). They carried out an investigation in a Californian school, which apparently demonstrated that randomly selected pupils whose teachers had been told they would make 'intellectual spurts', in fact subsequently demonstrated significant IQ gains compared with their classmates. This study has, however, been condemned as technically defective by Thorndike (1968) and Snow (1969) who, while not denying the credibility of the hypothesis which is being tested, find fault with the inadequacy of the research procedures and the inappropriateness of the conclusions drawn. Experimental studies attempting to demonstrate the influence of teacher expectation with individual children inevitably involve deliberately giving teachers misinformation. It has been suggested elsewhere, however, (Pidgeon, 1970) that the operation of the self-fulfilling prophecy through teacher expectations is nowhere more evident than in schools which stream or divide their pupils into homogeneous ability-groups, since teachers of high or low groups, aware of the intelligence level of their pupils, assume convictions about the possibility or impossibility of their level of learning.

If what teachers expect from their pupils does have an influence on what pupils do in fact learn, then concern with the factors that determine such expectations is not irrelevant. The point being stressed here is that teacher expectations are determined much more by the philosophical beliefs held than by the actual circumstances in which a particular teacher finds himself teaching. The kinds of changes taking place in the British primary school are mostly changes which demand a set of beliefs different from those which generally prevail among teachers in the more traditional formally structured school. The new approaches require not only different methods and techniques but a different philosophy. Without changes in what teachers believe about the education of children it is unlikely that any real differences will become apparent in either the cognitive or affective aspects of what pupils learn.

The beliefs about how children learn, on which the changed approach is largely based, are well set out in the Plowden Report (Central Advisory Council for Education, 1967, Vol. I, Chapter 16). They are easily understood, but perhaps not so readily accepted by many teachers who have become too entrenched in rather different philosophies. One of the greatest obstacles to acceptance is possibly the difficulty that many teachers experience in believing that an approach that does not seek to differentiate among children of clearly different abilities can indeed do justice to them all.

At this point, it is perhaps as well to distinguish between the cognitive and affective aspects of learning. Most people today would be prepared to accept the fact that education is concerned not only with the intellectual development of children but also with their physical, emotional, social, aesthetic and even moral development. 'A school is not merely a teaching shop, it must transmit values and attitudes' says the Plowden Report (paragraph 505). Teachers for the most part have little problem in accepting that the affective and conative aspects of learning are not only important but apply with equal force to all children. Few would deny that, irrespective of ability all children should be given the opportunity to 'be themselves, to live with other children and with grown ups, to learn from their environment, to enjoy the present, to get ready for the future, to create and to love, to learn to face adversity, to behave responsibly, in a word, to be human beings' (Plowden, paragraph 507). But cognitive learning is seen to be equally, if not more, important, and it is here that most teachers recognize that there are basic differences in children that cannot be ignored.

The problem, as most teachers view it, is that if children differ in ability, they cannot all be expected to reach the same levels in achievement. Just as children vary in intelligence, so do learning tasks vary in complexity, and the more intelligent a child, the more complex a task he is able to learn. Given that innate ability is approximately normally distributed, the expectation must be for achievement also to be normally distributed. Most teachers are prepared to believe that this is a true statement of reality because all the evidence of their own education and experience lends support to it. The distribution of achievement *is* normal; a few children (about ten per cent) learn most things with very little difficulty; equally a few (another ten per cent) have difficulty in learning even the simplest of tasks; the remainder are spread out in between, mostly around the average. Not only is this a statement of what happens when children tackle a new learning task, but it illustrates the accepted philosophy of traditional learning.

An alternative model for learning has been put forward by Carroll (1963) and elaborated by Bloom (1968 and 1971), in which aptitude for learning is related to the time required by a pupil to learn a given task. What the model says is that the degree of learning is a function, not of ability or aptitude *per se*, but of the extent to which a given pupil is able or willing to spend the time he needs in order to learn. Pupils will vary in the time they require to 'achieve mastery' as Bloom puts it, but whether they learn to master or not depends upon (a) whether they are prepared to spend the requisite amount of time needed, and (b) whether they are allowed to do so. Both these factors are under the control of the teacher, provided he is prepared to accept the basis on which the model is built. The former is related to motivation—any learning task must be presented in such a way that the pupil is intrinsically motivated, and not coerced into learning by some externally applied incentive. The latter depends upon the structural organization of the class and school. If a teacher, in order to 'cover the syllabus', is only prepared to let children spend a fixed amount of time on learning any particular task, inevitably there will be many for whom this is insufficient.

The shift in emphasis from teaching to learning and from dependence on extrinsic motivation is an essential part of the change in British primary schools. It is a change that can be visually witnessed. It does not of itself, however, involve the kind of attitudinal change implied by the Carroll learning model or by Bloom's concept of mastery learning. For a teacher to go along with Bloom, and believe that ninety to ninety-five per cent of his pupils are capable of learning even the most complex of tasks, involves a really fundamental attitudinal change. Most teachers, including many of those now teaching in the informal classroom, still need a great deal of convincing that ability *per se* is not the all-important attribute of learning, although they may well be prepared to accept with Bloom that the affective consequences of achievement cannot be neglected (Bloom, 1971). If low ability consistently results in failure to learn, this inevitably promotes a negative self-concept which itself induces yet more failure. To believe, however, that all that is needed for the successful learning of even complex tasks, by children of low ability, is good instruction and the appropriate amount of time, requires such a radical change of outlook that it cannot be expected to occur easily.

Bibliography

Barker Lunn, J. C. STREAMING IN THE PRIMARY SCHOOL
National Foundation for Educational Research
in England and Wales, Slough 1970; Fernhill House
Limited, New York

Block, J. H. MASTERY LEARNING: THEORY AND PRACTICE
Holt, Rinehart & Winston, London 1971

Bloom, B. S. STABILITY AND CHANGE IN HUMAN CHARAC-
TERISTICS John Wiley & Sons, New York 1964

Bloom, B. S. 'Learning for Mastery' EVALUATION
COMMENT UCLA 1968

Bloom, B. S. 'Individual Differences in School
Achievement: A Vanishing Point?' EDUCATION IN
CHICAGO 1971

Burstall, C. FRENCH FROM EIGHT: A NATIONAL EXPERI-
MENT National Foundation for Educational Research in England and Wales, Slough 1968; Fernhill House Limited, New York

Burstall, C. 'French in the Primary School: Some
Early Findings' JOURNAL OF CURRICULUM STUDIES
2.1 1970

Burt, C. 'Intelligence and Heredity: Some Common
Misconceptions' IRISH JOURNAL OF EDUCATION 3,2.
75–94 1969

Carroll, J. B. 'A Model of School Learning' TEACHERS
COLLEGE REVIEW 64 723–733 1963

CHILDREN AND THEIR PRIMARY SCHOOLS Central
Advisory Council for Education, London, HMSO
1967; Pendragon House, 899 Broadway Avenue,
Redwood City, California 94063

Coleman, J. S. EQUALITY OF EDUCATIONAL OPPORTU-
NITY US Government Printing Office, Washington
DC 1966

Cox, C. B. and Dyson, A. E. FIGHT FOR EDUCATION—A
BLACK PAPER Critical Quarterly Society, London
1969

Cox, C. B. and Dyson, A. E. BLACK PAPER TWO—THE CRISIS OF EDUCATION Critical Quarterly Society London 1969

Cox, C. B. and Dyson, A. E. BLACK PAPER THREE— GOODBYE MR SHORT Critical Quarterly Society London 1970

CURRENT RESEARCHES IN EDUCATION AND EDUCATIONAL PSYCHOLOGY 1968–69 NFER, Slough 1970: Fernhill House Limited, New York

Dale, R. R. 'An Analysis of Research on Comparative Attainment in Mathematics in Single-Sex and Co-educational Maintained Grammar Schools' EDUCATIONAL RESEARCH V. 1, 10–15, 1962

Daniels, J. C. 'Some Effects of Sex Segregation and Streaming on the Intellectual and Scholastic Development of Junior School Children'. Unpublished thesis, Nottingham University 1959

Eaglesham, E. S. R. THE FOUNDATIONS OF 20TH CENTURY EDUCATION IN ENGLAND Routledge & Kegan Paul London 1967; Humanities Press, New York

Finley, C. J. and Berdie, F. S. THE NATIONAL ASSESSMENT APPROACH TO EXERCISE DEVELOPMENT National Assessment of Educational Progress, Ann Arbor Michigan 1970

Goldberg, M. L., Passow, A. H. and Justman, J. THE EFFECTS OF ABILITY GROUPING Teachers College Press, New York 1966

Husen, T. INTERNATIONAL STUDY OF ACHIEVEMENT IN MATHEMATICS I & II Almqvist & Wiksell, Stockholm; John Wiley & Sons, London 1967

'Literacy Survey: Summary of interim results of the study of pupils' reading standards' Inner London Education Authority. Duplicated unpublished report 1969

Marburger, C. L. 'Considerations for Educational Planning' EDUCATION IN DEPRESSED AREAS (ed Passow, A. H.) Teachers College Bureau of Publications 1963

Merton, R. K. 'The Self-Fulfilling Prophecy' THE ANTIOCH REVIEW Summer 1948; SOCIAL THEORY AND SOCIAL STRUCTURE Free Press, New York revised and enlarged edition 1957

Peaker, G. F. 'Regression analysis of the National Survey' CHILDREN AND THEIR PRIMARY SCHOOLS Vol. II Appendix 4 London HMSO 1967; Pendragon House, 899 Broadway Avenue, Redwood City, California 94063

Peaker, G. F. PLOWDEN FOLLOW-UP NFER, Slough 1971; Fernhill House Limited, New York

Pidgeon, D. A. EXPECTATION AND PUPIL PERFORMANCE NFER, Slough 1970; Fernhill House Ltd, New York

PROGRESS IN READING Department of Education and Science, HMSO, London 1966: Pendragon House, 899 Broadway Avenue, Redwood City, California 94063

Ravitz, M. 'The Role of the School in the Urban Setting' EDUCATION IN DEPRESSED AREAS (ed. Passow, A. H.) Teachers College Bureau of Publications 1963

REPORT OF THE CONSULTATIVE COMMITTEE ON THE PRIMARY SCHOOL (Chairman: Sir W. H. Hadow) Board of Education 1931 HMSO, London; Pendragon House, 899 Broadway Avenue, Redwood City, California 94063

Rogers, V. R. TEACHING IN THE BRITISH PRIMARY school Collier-Macmillan, London and New York 1971

Rosenthal, R. and Jacobson, L. PYGMALION IN THE CLASSROOM Holt Rinehart & Winston, New York 1968

Snow, R. 'Review of "Pygmalion in the Classroom" by Rosenthal and Jacobson' CONTEMPORARY PSYCHOLOGY 14, 197–199 1969

Thorndike, R. L. 'Review of "Pygmalion in the Classroom" by Rosenthal and Jacobson' AERA JOURNAL V. 4, 708–711 1968

Wiseman, S. EDUCATION AND ENVIRONMENT Manchester University Press, 1964

Glossary

For a fuller understanding of some terms that are briefly defined in the following list, the reader is referred to one or more books in this series.

Cooperative teaching
Team teaching. An example of cooperative teaching is described in detail in A RURAL SCHOOL.

Eleven plus (11+)
Term used to cover the procedures and techniques (eg, attainment and/or intelligence tests, and teachers' reports) used by local education authorities mainly to select pupils for grammar schools at the age of 11; formerly in universal use, now decreasingly, and only in areas where selection continues. A view of the eleven plus is given in AN INTRODUCTION by Joseph Featherstone.

Family grouping
See **Vertical grouping**.

Grammar school
Academic High School.

Half-term
Mid-semester (see also **Term**).

Hall
Multi-purpose space, large enough to hold the whole school (staff and pupils). Usually a large room, often combining the functions of dining hall, auditorium and gymnasium.

Headteacher
Principal. For an examination of the headteacher's work, and the differences between headteachers and US principals, see THE HEADTEACHER'S ROLE and THE GOVERNMENT OF EDUCATION.

Health visitor
Qualified nurse with special training who is employed by the local education authority to visit schools to check on the children's health.

Her Majesty's Inspector (HMI)
Her Majesty's Inspector of Schools. Appointed formally by the Privy Council to advise the Department of Education and Science, and schools, on the practices and standards of education; and to maintain liaison between the DES and local education authorities. See also THE GOVERNMENT OF EDUCATION.

Infant school	School or department for children from five to seven or eight years old.
Integrated day	A school day in which children may pursue various interests or themes, without regard to artificial divisions into time periods. The workings of an integrated day are fully described in A RURAL SCHOOL.
Junior school	School for seven to eleven or twelve year olds.
Local education authority (LEA)	County or county borough council with responsibility for public education in its area. See THE GOVERNMENT OF EDUCATION.
Movement	An activity where the children explore expressive, agile, and games-like situations. This is done through the dynamic use of the body, with spatial orientation as it comes into contact with people and objects.
Primary school	School for children under twelve. It may be an **Infant school** or **Junior school** (*qq.v.*) or a combination of both.
School managers	Members of an appointed managing body of not fewer than six members who are representative of various interests concerned with the school. For a fuller explanation, and information on the powers and responsibilities of school managers, see THE GOVERNMENT OF EDUCATION.
School year	This begins in September and consists of three terms (see **Terms**).
Special classes	Remedial classes.
Standards I-VIII	Grades in the former Elementary Schools (for children from five to fourteen years).
Streaming	Tracking.
Teachers' centre	A centre set up by a local education authority to provide opportunities for curriculum development and associated in-service training for teachers. See EDUCATING TEACHERS.
Term	The English school year is divided into three terms (cf semesters): Autumn (Fall), Spring, and Summer.
Timetable	Schedule.
Tuition	Teaching. (In Britain, the word 'tuition' never has the meaning, 'fees'.)
Vertical grouping	(also called **Family grouping**): Form of grouping, found mainly in infant schools, in which the full age range for which the school provides may be represented in each class. See also SPACE, TIME AND GROUPING.